Gin Cookbook

Delicious Gin Recipes with Flavors that
will Knock you Out

BY

Carla Hale

Copyright 2019 Carla Hale

License Notes

No part of this Book can be reproduced in any form or by any means including print, electronic, scanning or photocopying unless prior permission is granted by the author.

All ideas, suggestions and guidelines mentioned here are written for informative purposes. While the author has taken every possible step to ensure accuracy, all readers are advised to follow information at their own risk. The author cannot be held responsible for personal and/or commercial damages in case of misinterpreting and misunderstanding any part of this Book

Table of Contents

Introduction 6

    Blackberry Apple Gin 8

    Simple Grapefruit Infused Gin 10

    Blueberry Rose Gin 12

    Raspberry Mint Gin 14

    Blackberry Ginger Gin 16

    Cucumber Rose Gin 18

    Blackberry Lavender Gin 20

    Peachy Keen Gin 22

    Strawberry Basil Gin 24

    Lemongrass Grapefruit Gin 26

    Watermelon Basil Gin Cocktail 28

    Simple Orange Zest Gin 30

    Midwinter Gin 32

    Orange Rhubarb Gin 34

Tamarind Orange Infused Gin 37

Elderberry Gin 39

Apricot Gin 41

Cherry Cinnamon Gin... 43

Ginger Lime Infused Gin 45

Caraway Cantaloupe Gin 47

Lychee Melon Gin 49

Blood Orange Infused Gin 51

Apple Pear Gin.. 53

Blackberry Lemon Shooters 55

Cucumber Infused Gin 57

Cranberry Herb Gin Cocktail.. 59

Nectarine Thyme Gin Cocktail 61

Clementine Gin Infusion... 64

Pomegranate Infused Gin.. 66

Simple Pear Gin 68

Conclusion 70

Author's Afterthoughts 71

About the Author 72

Introduction

Generally, clear liquors are best for infusing (gin, vodka, white tequila, etc.) If a liquor already has a color to it, most likely it has already been steeped and as a result, you will not get maximum flavor from the fruits and vegetables. Wine is the exception: red and white wine are perfect for simple and short-term infusions (also called sangrias).

Gin is one of the main categories of spirits. Any liquor whose predominant flavor is derived from juniper berries can be considered as gin. Since gin companies make their own gins, each brand may taste different. Some experimenting is needed to find out your preference. Once you have made your decision then you can decide what you put in it.

Gin cookbook is here to assist you with choosing the right, fruits, vegetables, herbs and spices to prevent a clash. For example, apples and strawberries are perfect together, infusing them with a basic gin would result in a delightful, fruity drink. Bear in mind, these mixtures are all subject to taste. It is always best to approach liquor infusions with an innovative, artistic approach rather than a scientific approach alone, although having some safety knowledge won't hurt.

Blackberry Apple Gin

This fruity gin will provide the kick needed to get your day done.

Serves: 12

Time: 5 mins.

Ingredients

- Gin (1, 750ml bottle)
- Blackberries (8 oz)
- Apples (8 oz, chopped)
- Bay leaf (1)
- Sugar (7 oz, caster)

Directions:

1. Place the blackberries, bay leaf, apples and sugar in a large sealable jar or other glass container.

2. Pour the gin over the ingredients and seal the container.

3. Shake well to ensure proper mixing and store in a cool, dark place for approximately 4 weeks, occasionally shaking every few days. You can also taste test to find preferred flavor.

4. Use a cheesecloth to strain the gin and rebottle the infused gin.

5. Serve with ice or with soda.

Simple Grapefruit Infused Gin

Add the citrusy flavor of grapefruit to your next glass of gin.

Serves: 12

Time: 10 mins.

Ingredients:

- Gin (1, 750ml bottle)
- Grapefruits (2, pink or red, zested, seeded, juiced)

Directions:

1. Combine the grapefruit juice and zest in a large sealable jar.

2. Pour the gin over the grapefruit and stir well.

3. Seal the jar and store in a cool, dark location for approximately 1 month.

4. After 1 month has elapsed, strain out the zest, and other fine particles, and rebottle the gin in a clean container.

5. Serve with ice and soda water for a nice, refreshing drink.

Blueberry Rose Gin

Blueberry goes well with alcohol as you will see in this blueberry gin.

Serves: 12

Time: 10 mins.

Ingredients:

- Gin (1, 750ml bottle)
- Blueberries (6 oz)
- Rose buds (1/2 oz, dried)

Directions:

1. Combine all the ingredients in a sealable glass container.

2. Seal the container and shake a few times to mix the infused gin.

3. Store for up to 9 days in a cool, dark place and ensure to check on the taste daily as well as to shake the container to release more flavor.

4. Serve in a cocktail with a rose as a garnish.

Raspberry Mint Gin

This Raspberry Mint Gin is easy to make and delicious.

Ingredients:

- Gin (1, 750 ml bottle)
- Raspberries (6 oz)
- Mint sprigs (3, fresh)

Directions:

1. Mix all the ingredients together in a clean, sealable airtight container.

2. Store for 5 days, shaking 1 to 3 days per day. Tasting daily to ensure flavor is to your liking.

3. Serve with tonic or over ice. A fresh mint leaf and fresh raspberries makes a great garnish.

Blackberry Ginger Gin

This blackberry and ginger combo make for an amazing drink.

Serves: 12

Time: 10 mins.

Ingredients:

- Gin (1, 750ml bottle)
- Blackberries (6 oz)
- Ginger (1/2 cup, sliced, peeled)

Directions:

1. Combine all the ingredients in a glass airtight container. Seal and shake a few times to mix the infusion.

2. Store for approximately 9 days in a cool, dark and secure place. Ensuring to taste it daily, as well as to shake it to release more flavor.

3. For a lesser taste of ginger, add the ginger 3 days after the blackberries.

4. When the flavor is to your liking, strain out the solids and rebottle the gin.

5. Serve over ice or in a tonic. Enjoy!

Cucumber Rose Gin

This cucumber rose mixture is simply delicious when done right.

Serves: 12

Time: 15 mins.

Ingredients:

- Gin (1, (750 ml) bottle)
- Cucumber (1, sliced)
- Rose buds (1/2 oz, dried)

Directions:

1. In a medium sized mason jar place all the ingredients.

2. Seal and shake a few times to agitate the infusion.

3. Store in a cool, dry place and shake for approximately 1 to 3 times each day. Also taste daily to check on flavor.

4. Next, strain through a cheesecloth when at desired flavor. Rebottle the infused booze and store in the refrigerator.

5. Serve over ice or in a tonic. A rose bud makes a pretty garnish.

Blackberry Lavender Gin

This dish is fragrant and just sweet enough.

Serves: 12

Time: 15 mins.

Ingredients:

- Gin (1, (750ml) bottle)
- Blackberries (6 oz)
- Lavender (2-3 sprigs, fresh)

Directions:

1. Place all the ingredients in a sealable glass container.

2. Seal the container and shake to agitate the infusion.

3. Store the container in a dark place for approximately 9 days.

4. After the 9th day has elapsed, remove the lavender.

5. Seal it up again and let the blackberries infuse for another 2 days.

6. Strain the infusion through a cheesecloth and rebottle the gin in a clean receptacle. Store in the refrigerator.

7. Serve over ice or in a tonic with a lavender sprig for garnish!

Peachy Keen Gin

This delicious drink will set you on edge with its huge flavors.

Serves: 2 – 4

Time: 15 mins.

Ingredients:

- Peaches (2, ripe, pitted and sliced)
- Gin (12 oz)

Directions:

1. Place the peach slices in a 16-ounce mason jar.

2. Cover the peaches with gin and seal the container. Shake a few times and store for approximately 2 to 5 days. Shake and taste daily to check on flavor.

3. Strain the peaches from the gin and rebottle the infused liquor. Store in the refrigerator.

4. Use the liquor-soaked peaches as garnish and serve over ice in a tonic.

Strawberry Basil Gin

Basil goes great with fruits and this mix is no different.

Serves: 4

Time: 15 mins.

Ingredients:

- Strawberries (1 cup, hulled and sliced)
- Basil (1/2 cup, chopped and tightly packed)
- Gin (1/2 bottle, enough to fill quart-sized container)

Directions:

1. Place the strawberries and basil in a quart-sized sealable container. Cover with the gin and fill almost to the top, leaving 1/4-inch of room.

2. Seal and shake a few times and store in a cool, dry place for approximately 1 week.

3. Check the flavor after the first few days. If you'd like more flavor, agitate the jar daily.

4. Strain out the solids and rebottle the gin. Keep in the refrigerator until ready to serve.

5. Serve in a tonic or over ice. A sliced strawberry makes a pretty garnish.

Lemongrass Grapefruit Gin

These tasty flavors are generally served as a tea but here we have a more adult version with the addition of gin.

Serves: 4

Time: 15 mins.

Ingredients:

- Grapefruit (1, large, peeled, pitted, segmented, cut into 1-inch pieces)
- Lemongrass (4, 5-inch stocks, each vertically cut in half)
- Lime (1, peeled and cut into 1-inch slices
- Gin (2 cups)

Directions:

1. In a sealable glass container, combine all the ingredients and stir gently.

2. Seal the container and place in a dark, cool location for approximately 5 days.

3. Shake and taste daily to ensure desired flavoring.

4. Strain out the solids, placing pressure on the grapefruit and lime slices in the strainer to expel more juice.

5. Rebottle the gin and discard the fruit. Store in your refrigerator until ready to serve.

6. Serve as a gin and tonic or just with ice!

Watermelon Basil Gin Cocktail

This tasty drink is great for lighter drinkers.

Serves: 1

Time: 5 mins.

Ingredients:

- Watermelon juice (1½-2 oz, freshly pressed)
- Cucumber (2 slices)
- Basil (3 leaves, torn, plus sprigs for garnish)
- Gin (1½ oz)
- Liqueur (1/2 oz, elderflower, or St. Germain)
- Sugar (1/2 tsp, raw)
- Lime (1/2, sliced in wedges for mudding)
- Splash of soda

Directions:

1. In a bowl or mixing tin, muddle the basil leaves, cucumber slices, sugar and lime wedges.

2. Add the watermelon juice, gin, and liqueur then a handful of ice. Stir or shake to ensure mixing.

3. To serve, pour into a tall glass and top off with a splash of soda.

4. A sprig of basil makes a fine garnish. Rub the basil between your hands to release more flavor.

Simple Orange Zest Gin

This lightly-flavored orange cocktail is a good way to cool down on a hot Summer night.

Serves: 6

Time: 15 mins.

Ingredients:

- gin (1 liter, enough to fill container)
- orange (1, just the peel in thin strips, pith should be removed)

Directions:

1. Get an airtight container, place gin and orange peel in. Seal lid and vigorously to mix.

2. Place in a cool, dark location for storage; up to 3 days. Check on flavor by tasting daily.

3. Serve over ice as a gin and tonic! Add a splash of soda to bring this already lively concoction to life.

Midwinter Gin

Just a sip of this tasty cocktail on a cold night will make you feel as if the sun is not far away.

Serves: 6

Time: 15 mins.

Ingredients:

- cranberries (250g; fresh)
- orange (1, just the peel in thin strips with the pith removed)
- gin (400ml, enough to fill container)

Directions:

1. Pierce the skins of the cranberries by using a knife or fork to release the flavor.

2. Place all the ingredients in an airtight container, seal, and shake to agitate flavor.

3. Store in a dark, cool location, ensure the infusion is checked daily. Shake and taste test. Store for up to 2 weeks.

4. When infusion has reached its peak flavor, strain and rebottle the gin in a clean container.

5. Serve over ice in a tonic!

Orange Rhubarb Gin

A cool way to enjoy Summer in the hot sunshine sipping on this Orange Rhubarb Gin.

Serves: 4

Time: 15 mins.

Ingredients:

- gin (2 cups)
- rhubarb (2 cups, chopped)
- orange (1, just the peel in thin strips with the pith removed)
- orange liqueur (2 tbsp., triple sec or Cointreau)
- dark brown sugar (1/4 cup, packed)

Directions:

1. In a saucepan, combine rhubarb and orange liqueur. Bring to a simmer for 2 minutes on low.

2. Transfer from heat and put aside to cool.

3. Fill a quart-sized sealable jar with all the ingredients. Seal and shake well to ensure mixing. Store in a cool, dark place for 4 to 5 weeks.

4. Shake and taste the infusion daily up to 3 days to find preferred level of flavor.

5. Strain using a mesh strainer or cheesecloth. Rebottle gin in a clean container.

6. Serve over ice or with soda.

Tamarind Orange Infused Gin

A rich flavored cocktail. It will leave you asking for more.

Serves: 6

Time: 10 mins.

Ingredients:

- gin (1 ½ cup gin)
- orange (1, half sliced and half just the zesty peel)
- sugar (2 tbsp.)
- tamarind flesh (1/3 cup)
- water (1/2 cup)

Directions:

1. In a saucepan, combine the tamarind flesh with 1/2 cup water. Heat to a boil and then bring the heat down and simmer for 3 to 4 minutes. The water should soak into the flesh and evaporate. Transfer from heat and put aside to cool.

2. Immediately as the tamarind is cooled, put all ingredients in a jar with a sealable lid. Seal and shake jar to mix.

3. Store in a cool location for up to 3 weeks. Check on the taste daily and shake to release more flavor.

4. Strain through a cheesecloth or mesh strainer. A coffee filter will catch the finer particles, if desired.

5. Serve with a tonic over ice!

Elderberry Gin

This recipe is the perfect way to use up those berries in your garden.

Serves: 1

Time: 15 mins.

Ingredients:

- gin (2 cups)
- elderberries (2 tbsp. dried or fresh)
- elder flowers (1/3 cup, dried)
- simple syrup (2 tbsp., to taste)

Directions:

1. Place all ingredients in an airtight container and seal.

2. Store for about 2 to 3 weeks. Shake every other day and taste daily to check on flavor.

3. Strain and filter out the solid particles. Rebottle gin and refrigerate until ready to serve.

4. Serve over ice with soda.

Apricot Gin

This gin is a perfect refreshing twist to your hot summer days. Surprise your husband, father or significant other with this tasty treat.

Serves: 8

Time: 10 mins.

Ingredients:

- gin (700 ml)
- apricots (700g, pitted and sliced)
- apricot pits (5; throw away the rest)
- sugar (100g)

Directions:

1. In a large sealable jar, pack together all the ingredients. Seal and shake to mix.

2. Store in a dark place shaking daily to ensure the sugar dissolves.

3. Taste after 2 or 3 months to check on flavor, strain out the solid particles.

4. Rebottle the gin in a clean container and refrigerate. Serve at your convenience.

5. Serve over ice or as a tonic!

Cherry Cinnamon Gin

This gin has a touch of class with its nice rich cherry taste and the cinnamon and cloves adding a touch of spice to its flavor.

Serves: 10

Time: 10 mins

Ingredients:

- gin (1 bottle)
- cherries (2 cups, fresh, pitted)
- superfine sugar (1 cup)
- cinnamon (1 stick)
- a few cloves (optional)
- almond extract (1 or 2 drops)

Directions:

1. Fill a sealable glass container with all the ingredients. Seal and store in a cool, dark place. Shake the jar to ensure thorough mixing.

2. Store for 2 weeks, shaking daily. Infuse for up to 3 months, tasting occasionally to check on flavor.

3. When the taste is to your suit, strain out the solid particles with a mesh strainer and a coffee filter. Rebottle infused gin.

4. Serve over ice or with tonic water.

Ginger Lime Infused Gin

A spectacular tasting liqueur. Its touch of lime, ginger and agave, gives it a spicy yet refreshing flavor.

Serves: 10

Time: 10 mins.

Ingredients:

- lime (1, half sliced and half just the zest without pith)
- 2 tablespoons chopped ginger, more or less
- 2 tablespoons agave syrup
- 2 cups gin

Directions:

1. In a sealable glass container, combine lime, ginger, and gin. Stir well, and seal the container and store in a cool, dark place for about 3 weeks.

2. After 3 weeks, add the agave syrup and let sit for another week. Taste to ensure desired flavor.

3. Strain and filter out the solid particles and rebottle the infused gin.

4. Serve over ice in a tasty cocktail.

Caraway Cantaloupe Gin

The flavor of cantaloupe in this recipe is strong yet tasty.

Serves: 4-6

Time: 15 mins

Ingredients

- 175 to 350ml dry gin
- 1 ripe cantaloupe, peeled and balled or finely chopped
- 1 tablespoon caraway seeds, lightly bruised with a mortar and pestle

Directions:

1. Place all ingredients in a sealable glass container. Seal and shake to mix.

2. Set aside in a cool, dark location for 2 to 3 weeks. Check on taste periodically. Shake more for more flavor.

3. Strain out the solids and rebottle the newly infused gin.

4. Serve with a tonic and a piece of cantaloupe for garnish.

Lychee Melon Gin

This melon and lychee combo is near to mind blowing.

Serves: 12

Time: 10 mins.

Ingredients:

- Gin (1 liter)
- Lychee fruit (1 lb., peeled)
- Melon (1 cup, honeydew, cubed or balled)

Directions:

1. Combine all the ingredients in an airtight container. Seal and shake to ensure mixing.

2. Store in a cool, dark location for approximately 2 to 3 weeks. Check on taste every few days. Shake the container if more flavor is desired.

3. Strain out the solid particles when level of flavor is achieved. Use a coffee filter for the finer particles.

4. Rebottle the gin and refrigerate until ready to serve.

5. Serve over ice or with tonic water.

Blood Orange Infused Gin

This recipe will introduce you to a whole new view of blood orange.

Serves: 12

Time: 15 mins.

Ingredients:

- Blood oranges (5, sliced)
- Gin (1 bottle, enough to fill container)

Directions:

1. Combine the gin and oranges in an airtight container and seal the lid closed. Shake a few times to mix and store in a cool location for approximately 4 days.

2. Shake the mixture at least once a day. Taste on the 4th day to check on flavor. Store longer for a stronger flavor.

3. Strain through a cheesecloth and then a coffee filter to remove solid particles.

4. Serve with tonic over ice.

Apple Pear Gin

These humble fruits create one delicious drink.

Serves: 10

Time: 15 mins.

Ingredients:

- Gin (1 bottle)
- Apples (4, red, sliced)
- Pear (1, sliced)
- Pears (1/4 lb., dried)

Directions:

1. Place the fruits at the bottom of a sealable container. Cover with the gin and put the lid on tight. Shake a few times to mix the infusion.

2. Store in a cool, dark location for 1 week, tasting for flavor. If it's not to your liking yet, store a bit longer, testing daily.

3. Strain out the fruit particles with a cheesecloth or mesh strainer. Use a coffee filter after to get the finer particles.

4. Rebottle gin in a clean container and store with other liquors.

5. Serve over ice in a cocktail. Use a slice of apple or pear as a garnish.

Blackberry Lemon Shooters

This drink is meant to be enjoyed all in one go.

Serves: 1

Time: 10 mins.

Ingredients:

- Gin (2 oz)
- Blackberries (4, fresh, more for garnishing)
- Lemon juice (1 oz, fresh)
- Syrup (1 oz, simple)
- Ice cubes (crushed)

Directions:

1. In a mortar or bowl, place the blackberries and pestle. Muddle thoroughly.

2. In a cocktail shaker, combine the gin, lemon juice, and simple syrup. Blend well.

3. Add the blackberries and shake again.

4. To serve, add some crushed ice to 4 tall shot glasses.

5. Evenly pour the cocktail divided into the shot glasses.

6. Top with a blackberry garnish and enjoy!

Cucumber Infused Gin

Cucumbers are not just for salad, it can also make delicious drinks.

Serves: 8

Time: 15 mins.

Ingredients:

- Cucumber (1, medium, thinly sliced)
- Gin (1 bottle, enough to fill container)

Directions:

1. Place the ingredients in an airtight container. Seal and shake to mix.

2. Store in a cool, secure place for 3 to 5 days, shaking daily to release more cucumber flavor.

3. Once the desired flavor is reached, strain out the cucumbers with a cheesecloth and discard the cucumber slices.

4. Rebottle the gin and use in martinis or other cocktails.

Cranberry Herb Gin Cocktail

This recipe uses rosemary to add an extra kick to your cranberry.

Serves: 10

Time: 15 mins.

Ingredients:

- Gin (1 bottle, enough to fill container)
- Rosemary (4-5 sprigs, fresh)
- Cranberries (2 cups, fresh+ more for garnishing)
- Lemon (1, juiced)

Directions:

1. Place the cranberries and the gin in a large mason jar, seal and store for 1 week.

2. Next, strain and rebottle the gin, discarding the cranberries.

3. Using a cocktail shaker, combine some rosemary and lemon. Muddle well.

4. Add 3-4 ounces of the cranberry infused gin to the shaker with a bit of ice.

5. Shake until frost appears on the cocktail shaker. Strain into a clean cocktail glass.

6. Garnish with a sprig of rosemary and a few cranberries.

Nectarine Thyme Gin Cocktail

Herb are great with gin. This recipe uses thyme to offset the sweetness of the nectarine.

Serves: 4

Time: 15 mins.

Ingredients:

- Gin (1 ½ oz)
- Lime (1, wedged)
- Syrup (1 ½ oz, thyme)
- Nectarine (1/2, pitted and sliced)
- Thyme (a few sprigs, fresh)
- Champagne or sparkling water (splash)
- Thyme syrup Ingredients
- Sugar (2 cups)
- Water (2 cups)
- Thyme (3-4 handfuls)

Directions:

1. Firstly, create the thyme syrup; combine the sugar and water in a saucepan. Heat until sugar completely dissolves. Remove from heat and add the thyme.

2. Cover syrup while it's cooling and give it at least 1 hour to completely cool.

3. Remove and discard the thyme by straining. Set aside to use in the cocktail.

4. Using a cocktail shaker, combine the nectarine slices, lime wedges and thyme syrup. Muddle thoroughly with a wooden spoon.

5. Add the gin and the ice cubes and shake well.

6. To serve, place a few ice cubes in each glass and divide cocktail into glasses.

7. Top off with champagne or sparkling water. Garnish with a slice of nectarine or a sprig of thyme.

Clementine Gin Infusion

This clementine infusion is like no other.

Serves: 12

Time: 10 mins.

Ingredients:

- Gin (1 bottle, dry)
- Clementine (3, sliced + wedges for garnish)
- Salt (2 pinches, kosher)

Directions:

1. Combine all the ingredients in a quart-sized mason jar.

2. Seal the jar and let infuse for a minimum of 24 hours at room temperature.

3. Strain out the solid particles and rebottle the gin in a clean container.

4. Serve with sparkling white wine or tonic water.

Pomegranate Infused Gin

Here is an easy and tasty way to use pomegranate.

Serves: 12

Time: mins.

Ingredients:

- Gin (1, (750ml) bottle)
- Pomegranate (1, Seeds only)

Directions:

1. Firstly, place the pomegranate seeds at the bottom of a large mason jar with lid.

2. Cover with the gin and seal. Shake the jar a few times to ensure mixing.

3. Store in a cool, dark place for approximately 2 weeks, maybe up to 1 month.

4. When the gin becomes a deep pink color, strain out the pomegranate seeds and rebottle gin in a clean container.

5. Serve in a cocktail or add pomegranate juice for extra taste.

Simple Pear Gin

This humble pear gin is sweet and delicious.

Serves: 10

Time: mins.

Ingredients:

- Pears (2-3, sliced)
- Gin (1 bottle, enough to fill a quart-sized mason jar)

Directions:

1. Pour the gin over the sliced pears in a quart-sized mason jar. Seal and thoroughly shake.

2. Store in a dry, dark room for approximately 3 to 5 days. Taste occasionally to find preferred flavor.

3. When the desired flavor is achieved, strain out the solid particles using a mesh strainer and coffee filter.

4. Rebottle gin and use in cocktails with ice.

Conclusion

We are elated that you were able to complete all 30 delicious Gin recipes for the whole family. The next step from here is to continue practicing until you have perfected each one. After that, you can always find another amazing journey to partake in from cuisines across the globe in another one of our books. We hope to see you again soon. Happy cooking!

Author's Afterthoughts

Thanks Ever So Much to Each of My Cherished Readers for Investing the Time to Read This Book!

I know you could have picked from many other books but you chose this one. So, big thanks for buying this book and reading all the way to the end.

If you enjoyed this book or received value from it, I'd like to ask you for a favor. Please take a few minutes to post an honest and heartfelt review on **Amazon.** Your support does make a difference and helps to benefit other people.

Thank you!

Carla Hale

About the Author

Carla Hale

I think of myself as a foodie. I like to eat, yes. I like to cook even more. I like to prepare meals for my family and friends, I feel like that's what I was born to do…

My name is Carla Hale and as may have suspected already, I am originally from Scotland. I am first and foremost a mother, a wife, but simultaneously over the years I became a proclaimed cook. I have shared my recipes with many and will continue to do so, as long as I can. I like different. I dress different, I love different, I speak different and I cook different. I like to think that I am different because I am more animated about what I do than most; I feel more and care more.

It served me right when cooking to sprinkle some tenderness, love, passion, in every dish I prepare. It does not matter if I am preparing a meal for strangers passing by my cooking booth at the flea market or if I am making my mother's favorite recipe. Each and every meal I prepare from scratch will contain a little bite of my life story and little part of my heart in it. People feel it, taste it and ask for more! Thank you for taking the time to get to know me and hopefully through my recipes you can learn a lot more about my influences and preferences. Who knows you might just find your own favorite within my repertoire! Enjoy!

Printed in Great Britain
by Amazon